THE VAMPYRE COOKBOOK

...I know there is a vampire cook book...I have read pages from it...it has recipe's that contain garlic and onions as well as messages for blood pudding and blood sausage...It is a ghoulish recipe book for humans...

...whereas the one we have here is an alchemical book exclusively for vampyres...

LEAH BARROWS

PIRAAS PUBLISHING LLC
PO BOX 3093
ALEXANDRIA, VA 22302

THE VAMPYRE COOKBOOK
Copyright 2009 by Leah Barrows

All Rights Reserved

No part of this book may be reproduced in any manner whatsoever, through any means without permission except in the case of brief quotations embodied in critical articles or reviews. For more information contact PIRAAS Publishing, PO Box 29047, Washington, D.C., 20017. (www.piraaspublishing.com)

Illustrations and graphic art provided by Leah Barrows.

Cover Design by Dennis T. Comer

Barrows, Leah

    A Vampyre Cookbook/Leah Barrows

    1. Cookbook 2. Vampire 3. Goth 4. Fantasy

ISBN: 978-0-9767408-5-8 ; 0-9767408-5-0

Library of Congress Cataloguing Number: 2009901300

The eating of raw or uncooked meat, poultry and shellfish may be harmful. Neither the publisher nor the author take any responsibility for the recipe's contained herein.

DEDICATION

This book is dedicated to those who are unafraid to
love...

So you claim to be a Vampyre…one of the children of Lilith, do you?

I'm not here to judge you or persuade you to follow in the true ways of our kinds cuisine. I'd just ask that perhaps you should just stay out of the damn sunlight and try to avoid fruits and veggies that represent good old sunshine. I hate to be the bearer of bad news but that does include orange juice and lemons. We don't want to eat that which kills us, do we. I'd rather not.

As you venture into the true depths of the cuisine of the darkside, there are many toxic combinations that you must keep in mind. No garlic, no scallions, no basil and no tomatoes. These are the spices used in cultures from Egyption to Hindu, all of which for our demise…to kill vampires. In Italian black magic, the tomato is still used to banish demons and vampires.

Avoid red wines and foods with a high sulfur content.

The long term use of plants and ingredients with a high sulfur content could prove to be deadly. An example of some of these are cabbage, broccoli, spinach and garlic, to name a few.

I would say avoid nightshade plants as well but allergies to nightshade vary from species to species.

"Nightshade" is actually the common name used to describe over 2,800 types of plants. Your best bet would be to avoid the following forms of nightshade eggplants, black cherries, spinach and tomatoes. Some of these recipes do contain some verities nightshade so if you are sensitive (which you probably are) use your own discretion. Steaming, boiling, and baking can help reduce the toxicity of nightshades. Sometimes nightshade foods also contain low amounts of nicotine.

You have been informed. I take no responsibilities and absolve myself from anything that may occur while ingesting any of the ingredients and or recipes. However, if you end up with improved super powers or deluusions of super powers.

Please do not blame me.

CONTENTS

APPETIZERS

Carnivore	8
Tartar	8
Samurai Vlad	9
Spicy Samurai Vlad	10
Mermaid Tartar	11
Kali's Kids	12
Lupine Lust	12
Chicken Tartar	13

SOUPS AND STEW

Xiang Shi Soup	15
The Red Haired Vampire Soup	16
Cold Blood Soup	17
Sweet Succulent Strawberry Soup	18
Vengeful Vischyssoie	18
Ghoul Gumbo	19
Unseelie Court Stew	20
Dumpling Dough	20
Unseelie Court Stew 2	21
Red Cap Stew	21
Succubus Beef Stew	22
Creamy Potato Soup	23
Lady Bathory Bouillabaisse	24
Aztec Chocolate Soup	25

ENTREE's

Bloody Chili	26
Tangy Terrified Chicken	27
Venomous Vindaloo	28
Next Door Neighbor Surprise	29
Fairy Pig Dancing in a Meadow	30
Jaundiced Swine	31

Crab Cakes	32
Fig-etabout it Chicken	33
Decaying Duck	33
Luciferian Lobster	34
Crabs from Hell	34
Rockin' Ruby Red Chicken	35
Taste Like Human Meatloaf	36
Black Death Eggs	36

DRINKS AND SPIRITS

Changling Chai	38
Goth Girl Mellow Tea	39
Hibiscust Tea	39
Rotten Graveyard Coffee	40
Black Death Coffee	41
Incubus Iced Tea	42
Apricot Cider	42

DESSERTS AND OTHER DARK TREATS

Sorbet	44
Lavendar Ice Cream	44
Honey & Yogurt Ice Cream	44
Moon Melon Sorbet	45
Pomegranite Ice	45
Ginger Ice Cream	46
Real Ripe Red Rasberry Sorbet	47
Dracula Sorbet	47
Vetala Sorbet	48
Count VonCocoSteinbabe Cake	49
Pound of Flesh Cake	50
Ginger Bread Human	51
Coagulated Blood	52

APPETIZERS

...a bloody tidbit before you begin stalking your prey...

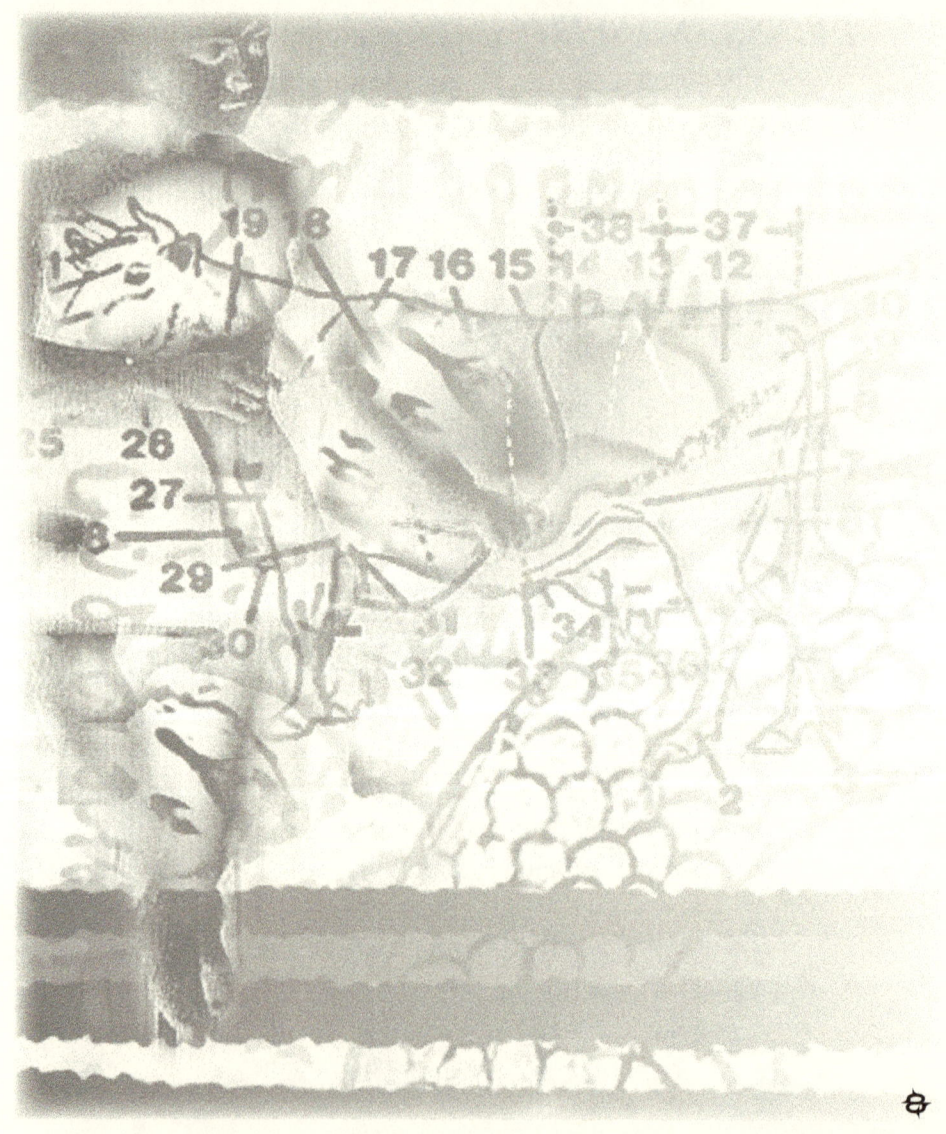

CARNIVORE - căr ° nĭ ° vöör; A meat eater, a consumer of flesh. A creature that consumes the souls of other living creatures. An earth dweller.

These are the words used to describe a species of creature on this planet. Does this embody the definition of evil? Perhaps it's just how a species chooses to eat...who knows...better yet...who cares? Let us prepare one of my favorites.

TARTAR

To make the best quality of tartar it is important to start with the best and freshest cuts of meat; use a filet mignon cut in regards to beef and the underbelly in regards to the cut of fish.

Always rinse the meat (fish or beef) in a bowl filled with half ice and half water.

All cuts, after being prepared, should be served immediately on chilled plates.

How to make a chilled plate:

Get some stoneware plates (stoneware keeps holds the temperatures best). Lightly spritz (or wipe with a damp cloth) the face of the plate with water.

Place plate in the freezer for about 20-30 minutes.

Hint: Do this before you prepare the tar tar. Remove plates when you are ready to serve.

Samurai Vlad

Vlad the impaler was a Romanian ruler who had a habit of killing a lot of people. He also was a samurai that could make steak tartar with amazing speed.

1 lb. filet mignon thinly sliced
1/2 Tablespoon sake
1/2 teaspoon sugar
4 dashes hot pepper sauce (Tabasco sauce) to taste
Kosher salt to taste
Freshly ground black pepper to taste
1 teaspoon paprika
dash allspice

Don't use any other grade of beef.
Lightly sift the sugar then mix sake with the sugar. Mix together all ingredients lightly. Place steak tartar on chilled plates and serve immediately.

Spicy Samurai Vlad

Vlad was a samurai vampire. It's TRUE... I read it somewhere in a cookbook I think.

1 Lb. filet mignon thinly sliced
1 Tablespoon Plum wine
1/4 teaspoon white pepper
1/2 teaspoon paprika
1/2 teaspoon fresh finely ground ginger
1/4 teaspoon wasabi
1/2 teaspoon brown sugar
2 dashes of Hot sauce
1 teaspoon kosher salt
Handful of Alfalfa sprouts

Sift the sugar. Mix all the spices and salt with the sugar. Slowly add the plum wine. Add this mixture to the steak. Garnish with Alfalfa sprouts (it looks pretty) Serve immediately. Your guests are now impressed...so eat!

Mermaid Tartar

Some say mermaids are a hybrid between water nymphs and vampires. Mermaids were known for leading swimmers and sailors to their death and then devouring their flesh once drowned. What? You don't believe in mermaids? Then why do you believe in vampires? This tastes good.

1/2 lb Salmon (the underbelly section used for sushi), thinly sliced
1 Lb. Filet Mignon (the good stuff), thinly sliced
1/2 teaspoon freshly chopped cilantro
Fresh black pepper
Dash allspice
1/4 teaspoon miso bean paste
1/2 Tablespoon Sweet Plum wine
1/4 teaspoon brown sugar
garnish with edible silver
1/4 cup sliced lettuce

Kali's Kids

The Hindi name for a vampire is called a Vetala. I call them Kali's Kids.

Dash of hot sauce
1/4 teaspoon ghee
1/2 tablespoon Mango Chutney
1/2 teaspoon fresh cilantro
1 ts kosher salt
1 lb filet mignon thinly sliced

Mix all the ingredients and serve immediately. Chopped beef should be freshly ground just before serving. It is served raw.
Serve on chilled plates. Eat immediately.

Lupine's Lust

Serve this when you invite your werewolf friends over and you want to tease them.

1/2 thinly sliced sweet red bell pepper
1 LB filet mignon
1 tablespoons finely sliced dried unsulfured apricots
1/4 teaspoon balsamic vinegar
1/4 teaspoons minced unsulfured black currants
1/4 cup shredded carrots
1/4 teaspoon kosher salt
2 3X3 edible silver flakes
Dash of hot sauce

Mix the entire ingredients. Place steak tartar on chilled plated and serve immediately.

Don't tell them about the silver: let them find out!

Chicken tartar

This is a recipe for chicken tartar.
From what I know about preparation of food and food handling, there is no such thing. It is unhealthy to eat chicken raw, unless you are a fox and have come across a really accessible hen house. Then it is ok.

1 Non existent chicken
1 Cup of do not eat

This is the end of the tartar section - on to the other foods yummm.

SOUPS & STEWS

The Immortal Chicken

Xiang shi soup

Some people are afraid of being bitten by a vampire, others are afraid of becoming an immortal. This soup is for them.

8 cups water
2 Tablespoons Kosher salt
1 whole chicken about 2-3lbs
4 slices fresh ginger the size of a thumb
3 large white potatoes cubed
1/4 teaspoon gotu kola
1 teaspoon Korean ginseng
2 bay leaves
1 tablespoon chopped cilantro
2 pinches of powdered myrrh
5 small Szechwan wild peppers

Preheat the oven to 350 degrees.
Clean the damned chicken. Using a cleaver cut/hack the chicken, through the bones, into 8 pieces. Place the chicken pieces and all ingredients, except the salt and cilantro,
in a heatproof iron pot. Cover tightly with heavy-duty aluminum foil and place the soup in the oven. Cover with a lid. Cook for 3 hours checking and stirring on occasion. Half an hour before the chicken is done add the salt and cilantro.

Remove the ginger and serve in bowls not champagne glasses...Wait!! Do not serve, you are afraid to. Calmly call one of your guests into the kitchen to admire your hard work.

The Red Haired Vampire Soup

People with red hair in many cultures were considered Vampires.

This is a delicious carrot soup. Served cold.

3 cups fresh carrot juice
1/4 cup shredded carrots
1 small cucumber (Remove seeds., but you can keep the skin on if you want to)
1 large avocado
2 3x3 edible gold flakes
1/2 teaspoon cilantro leaves
1/2 teaspoons kosher salt or to taste
1 teaspoon pomegranate juice (yes, pomegranates are your friend)

Find a vampire or demon with red hair, chain them in your cellar, then Measure 4 cups fresh carrot juice. Cut avocado in half, peel and remove pit. Place carrot juice, cucumber and avocado in blender, and blend until smooth.
Then garnish with the shredded carrots.

Serves 4 or 2 very greedy people.

When I was young I had red hair and hated the nickname carrot top. For you see a carrot top is green and not red. In order to demonstrate this from the pantry I would get green food coloring and carry a picture of a carrot with me.

The unfortunate evil playmate that was ignorant enough to tease me would receive a healthy amount of green food coloring dosed upon their unsuspecting heads. I would then leave a picture of a carrot and run away.

Coldblood Soup

A lot of vampires do not like this soup served cold. Use your own discretion.

3 cups fresh carrot juice
1 (12 or 14 oz can) of Roasted red peppers
2 3x3 edible gold flakes
1/2 teaspoon hot sauce (Tabasco)
1/4 teaspoons kosher salt
2 teaspoons pomegranate juice
dash of allspice
1/4 teaspoon miso bean paste

Blend carrot juice and entire contents of canned red peppers add all ingredients except gold flakes. That's your garnish, silly. Serves 6 very greedy people.

Sweet Succulent Strawberry Soup

2 pt strawberries
1/4 c sugar
1/4 c honey
2 cup cream, heavy
2 cup milk
pinch of myrrh
edible gold flakes

Chill soup bowls.

Cut stems off fresh berries or thaw frozen berries and rinse under cold water. In a food processor, puree the berries with the sugar, let it sit overnight. Whip heavy cream until thickened, but not stiff. Fold together thickened cream, milk and berry mixture. Pour the soup into chilled soup bowls, garnish with the edible gold, then serve.

Vengeful Vichyssoise

Gold in Egypt was a popular food of the immortals as were grapes in Greece. Melons are known to be fruit of the moon so the combination makes this delightful soup.

Revenge is soup best served cold

6 cups small cubes cantaloupe or honeydew melon
1/2 cup white grape juice
3 Tablespoons honey
1/4 cup unsweetened yogurt
6 ice cubes
3/8 in. x 3 24k gold leaf flakes
sliced strawberries

Heat grape juice in a pan bring to a boil. Then add 4 cups of melon. Remove from heat. Let sit 10 minutes. In a blender or food processor, combine melon mixture with honey, yogurt and six ice cubes add the remaining melons and blend until smooth. Chill. Garnish with sliced strawberries and gold flakes. Please use only 23k and 24k gold flakes known as "edible gold". Some bakery supply stores carry this delicacy, but it is not too expensive and will add an extra zing to your meal.

Ghoul Gumbo

1/4 cup crab meat (or diced imitation crab)
1 chicken breast cubed
1 lb. shrimp in shells
2 quarts water
2 bay leaves
1 cup cranberry juice
Dash of salt
red and black pepper
parsley
1/2 lb. okra
1 small zucchini chopped
1 tbs.. butter
2 sweet yellow peppers, finely chopped
2 green peppers, finely chopped
reserved shrimp stock
white pepper to taste
hot boiled rice

In a large iron pot, boil the water with bay leaves, and judicious amounts of salt, pepper and cayenne. Wash shrimp and add to pot; boil for 2 minutes. Peel shrimps and return shells to the stock for later use. Set shrimp and crab meat aside.

Sauté okra slices in large black skillet. The okra will turn darker and lose some of its stickiness as it cooks. When soft, transfer to a stew pot and add zucchini. Stir and mix together well. Sauté the green pepper and red peppers. When soft, add 2 cups of the shrimp stock to the stew pot. When well blended, add to the large stew pot with cranberry juice and other ingredients. Simmer for 2 hours, adding more strained stock if needed for consistency. Adjust seasonings with the salt, pepper, and parsley. When it has simmered for at least 3 to 4 hours, add the shrimp and crab meat and cook for 15 more minutes. Serve with fresh boiled rice in soup bowls. Serves 6 to 8.

Unseelie Court Stew

The Unseelies are the darker realm of the fae. Some drink blood and play practical jokes. You might say they are like the vampire cousin you wish you never knew. Some Faeries love apples. Apples are symbols of immortality of the underworld.

I am sure you can find some pixie stealing blue berries from a patch whatever you do, do not stop them leave them be, and never ask them for directions.

Dumpling Dough

2 Tablespoons shortening
1 Tablespoons butter
1 1/2 cups flour
2 teaspoons baking powder
1/2 teaspoon salt
3/4 cup milk

set aside then make:
1/2 Cup brown sugar
1/2 cup white sugar
1/4 Cup Cranberry Juice
1/4 cup diced dried apricots
4-Granny smith apple cubed
1 pint blueberries
dash of cardamom
dash of cinnamon

In a bowl, mix flour, baking powder and salt. Rub in shortening and butter with fingers. Stir in milk to make a soft dough. boil water. Reduce heat to a simmer and stir in sugar until dissolved. Stir in blueberries. Drop dough by rounded spoonfuls into simmering blueberry syrup. Drop in dumplings by the tablespoon and cook 10 minutes uncovered and 10 minutes covered, stirring occasionally. Cover and simmer for 5 minutes. Serve

Unseelie Court Stew 2

It rhymes and I could not think of another name.

4 cups fresh blackberries
1/2 cup granulated sugar
1/2 cup honey
1/2 cup Pomegranate juice
1 tsp. vanilla extract

Garnish with gold and silver flakes and a dollop (1/2 teaspoon) of ghee.

Red Cap Stew

The Red caps were mystical creatures known for killing people and then dying their hats with there blood. (What a waste of food) This is a good soup, when you add the dumplings it gives you the effect of floating heads in blood. Yumm.

First Prepare the Dumpling Dough

2 Tb. Shortening
1 Tb butter
1 1/2 cups flour
2 tsp salt
3/4 cup milk

Set aside:

1/2 Brown sugar
1 cup white sugar
1/2 cup cranberries
1/4 cup unsulfured yellow raisins
1 pint Raspberries
dash of chili pepper
3x3 gold flakes for garnish

In a deep skillet, boil water. Reduce heat to a simmer and stir in sugar until dissolved. Stir in cranberries. Let cook 10 minutes then add Raspberries. Let simmer for 5 minutes then add raisins. Drop dough by rounded spoonfuls into the syrup and cook 10 minutes uncovered and 10 minutes covered.

Succubus Beef Stew

Succubi were known to eat men, devouring their souls.

Instead of devouring a beefy guy, why not just a beef stew?

3 pounds lean beef, round or rump thinly sliced
2 tablespoons butter or Ghee
1/2 teaspoon kosher salt
1 bay leaf
6 small whole carrots
1 zucchini cubed
2 large potatoes cubed
1 sweet potato cubed
2 Tablespoons unsweetened Pomegranate juice

Cut meat into small pieces. Brown in fat. Add water to cover and seasonings. Simmer, covered, about 2 hours. Add vegetables and simmer until vegetables are tender, about 30 minutes. Then add Pomegranate Juice. Serve, yumm.

Serves 6-8.

Creamy Potato Soup

This is soup for the humans when they visit.

No fancy story or title this is just creamy potato soup.

So there!

1 cups diced peeled red russet potatoes
1 sweet potato peeled and cubed
1 teaspoon fresh ginger
1 1/2 cups water
1/2 teaspoon kosher salt
1/2 teaspoon sugar or honey

Cook above ingredients until tender. Mash (do not drain).

Then add:

2 Tbs. butter
1 cup milk

Bring ingredients to a simmer and stir continuously until mixture thickens. Reduce heat
then add:

1/2 cup of cream.

Remove from heat and stir.
Garnish with parsley and serve.

Lady Bathory Bouillabaisse

Lady Bathory was a noble woman who used to bathe in the blood of her maid servants.
In those days they did not have unions so working for her was temporary employment.

What is bouillabaisse? Glad you asked.

Bouillabaisse is a fancy French name for a type of soup.

Still do not know? Bouillabaisse is a very very fancy French name for soup.

1/2 lb chopped fish deboned ok no bones...no bones about it
1/4 lb lamb finely sliced
2 1/2 pints water
1 orchard apple or Granny Smith peeled and thinly sliced
3-4 tablespoons olive oil
2 tablespoon pimento
12 or 14 oz can roasted red peppers
1/4 teaspoon nutmeg
1lb pounds mixed filled fish (chopped)
3 pinches saffron
1/2 cup cranberry juice
10 shrimp or 15 if you don't want to be stingy
1/2 tablespoons Cilantro
1 teaspoon kosher salt

Clean the fish and place in a saucepan along with the water and spices. Boil rapidly for 15-20min Add the pimento, nutmeg and cook for a few minutes. Increase the heat and add lamb simmer for 20 minutes.

Puree the roasted red peppers and cranberry juice and add. Then add the saffron shrimp and cilantro immediately remove from heat. Cover for five minutes. Then Serve will serve 4 or six if you ration it well.

Aztec Chocolate Soup

The ancient Aztec priests would drink cocoa before sacrificing their victims. I just figured it would be a nice way to start a busy day.

2 cups milk
1 cup heavy whipping cream
1 tablespoons unsweetened cocoa powder
5 cubes bitter sweet chocolate
1/2 cup white sugar
1/2 teaspoon vanilla extract
1/4 teaspoon ground cinnamon
Dash of black pepper
1/4 teaspoon of chili pepper

Mix the cocoa, sugar, vanilla, cinnamon and milk and cocoa mixture.

Heat on low heat stirring continuously then add cubes of chocolate stir until melted then add cream. Remove from heat when all of the cubes have melted. Pour in to mugs or
soup bowls.

Serves the last 2 people remaining at the table.

ENTREE'S

Bloody Chili

2 pounds lean ground beef
1 Teaspoon fresh ginger
1 can (12-14 ounce) roasted red peppers
4 teaspoons chili powder
1 can (8-12 ounce) red kidney beans (Kidneys filter the blood)
1/2 tablespoons red vinegar
1 teaspoon kosher salt
Dash black pepper

In a large skillet add the ground beef, salt and ginger cook until meat is browned. In a blender blend roasted red peppers and add it to the chili. Let simmer for 10 minutes then add kidney beans, and vinegar. Mix well and simmer for 1 hour. This chili recipe will serve 6.

Tangy Terrified chicken

1/2 cup of plum wine
1/4 cup chopped carrots
2 large white potatoes chopped
3 Lb.. boneless, skinless chicken breasts sliced
1 cup olive oil
1 tsp. fresh cilantro
Salt and pepper to taste
2 cups plain unsweetened yogurt
1 cup water

Preheat the oven to 375. Violently and repeatedly stab the chicken.

Mix all of the above ingredients except the water. Let the chicken marinate overnight in the refrigerator.

Add water to the mixture. Let cook 1 hour or until done. That is it, there is no more.

Venomous Vindaloo

There is a story that the Indians created Vindaloo to drive out the colonizing British. It didn't work, but still, it can be a tasty way to scare your friends.

2 Granny Smith Apples Peeled (you know the green kind)
2 lb Chicken Breast
2 lb Chicken Thigh
2 1/2 Teaspoons Kosher Salt
1/4 C Ghee
1 1/2 teaspoons crushed coriander seed
1 teaspoon ground turmeric
1/2 teaspoon ground ginger
1/4 teaspoon ground cardamom
1 teaspoon paprika
pinch ground cumin
pinch cinnamon
1/4 teaspoon black pepper
1/8 teaspoon cayenne
1/2 Cup red vinegar
1 cup hot water

Clean the chicken. That means remove the feathers and entrails. Eat the fat or smear it on leather Jacket for shine. Remove excess fat. Stab the chicken repeatedly with a fork and rub in salt. While the chicken is cooking melt the ghee in a large skillet. Stir in 1 1/2 cups hot water, simmer, covered, for 35 minutes. Place the chicken in the sauce and cover and simmer for 1 hour.

Will serve 4 or the remaining guests that you let live.

Next Door Neighbor Surprise

The title does not warrant any further description nor discussion.

6 loin pork chops 1in thick or boneless chicken thighs,(Loin means no bone got it!! Bones leave evidence.)
1/4 cup chopped almonds (for that crunchy cartilage and bone feeling.)
1 tbs. butter (not margarine)
1/4 cup soft bread crumbs 1/2 cup butter crackers (Ritz is good.)
1 cup dried cranberries
1 tbs. brown sugar
1/2 tsp ginger
1/4 cup apricot preserves

Preheat oven to 350 degrees. That means let the oven heat for about 20 min. No short cuts, this is pork we are talking about. Slice deep pockets in the loin. (deeper than the cheap bastard's wallet for paying back the money he never repaid). In medium skillet, cook the almonds and cranberries for about 10 min. on medium heat. Then mix in all the remaining ingredients except for the apricots. Stuff each chop with about 1/4 cup of the mixture. Place in ungreased 13 x 9 inch baking dish, add 3 tablespoons of water to the pan. Cover, then bake for 30 min. Then drizzle apricot preserves over the top. Re-cover then bake for another 20 minutes. Be sure to share the meal with his wife and kids because they have been looking for him and you may feel a tad bit guilty.

Fairy Pig Dancing in a Meadow

In order to prepare this meal you must first find a fairy pig being surrounded by fairies carrying flowery garlands on a midsummers eve. As the fairies are singing and dancing with the animal, you go grab a mallet, and begin beating the pig senseless...sending fairies running and screaming away in horror and dismay *or* you can simply go to the market and purchase the following:

2 lb cooked ham, thinly sliced
12 oz cherries, dark sweet (can)
5 tsp cornstarch
1/4 cup light brown sugar
2 tbs. white vinegar
1/8 tsp cinnamon
1/8 tsp nutmeg
1/8 tsp Allspice
1/4 cup Hibiscus tea (recipe is in the book look for it)
2 tablespoons chopped marigolds

Place ham slices in a baking dish. Drain cherries, setting the syrup aside. Combine cherry syrup in saucepan with cornstarch, sugar, vinegar, water and spices. Cook over medium heat, stirring constantly, until thick and clear.

Add tea and cherries to the syrup mixture. Pour over ham slices and bake at 350F for 45 minutes. Garnish with marigolds before serving and chuckle.

Jaundiced Swine

During the black plague some vampires could no longer rely on the blood of humans because it probably tasted pretty disgusting, an occasional ill fed animal could be found wandering the filthy street. Yummy.

3 teaspoons turmeric
4 medium ripe mangoes (Mangoes are not native to Europe but we're international vampires here, aren't we?)
1 pound pork tenderloin or chicken thighs if pork aint your thing…
Olive oil
White pepper
Pinch of Kosher salt

Slice 2 mangos and puree in a blender. Cube the other mangoes. Cut pork cut into 1/2 inch slices. Beat it with a mallet. Heat pan on medium high with olive oil. Brown pork for 1 minute on each side, then add turmeric, salt and pepper.

Reduce heat and cook pork another 5 minutes to cook thoroughly. Transfer to a plate and add mango puree to pan. Cook puree about 30 seconds scraping up brown bits of pork as it cooks. Add the cubed mango and puree. Cover and remove from heat let sit about 5 minutes, then serve with rice. Serves 2.

Crab Cakes –

What? You have never heard of crab cakes before? Were you expecting something obscene?

1 1/2 pound crab meat
1 egg, lightly beaten and severely chastised
1 teaspoon kosher salt
1 yolk of an egg
1/2 Tablespoon curry (get the good stuff at the Indian store)
Cayenne pepper to taste
2 tbs. minced parsley
4 tbs. mayonnaise
2 Tables spoon diced cilantro
1 1/2 cup bread crumbs
1/4 cup avocado oil (go get some if you don't have any, ok unless you are allergic then 1 Tablespoon of butter with 1/4 cup vegetable oil might do)

In a large mixing bowl mix together the crab, egg, curry, cayenne, parsley, mayonnaise. Mix well, using your hands, and taste and correct seasonings as you are mixing the cakes.

Pat the crab mixture into about 10-12 small cakes. Spread the crumbs on a piece of wax paper. Heat oil in a large pan over medium heat. Coat the cakes in crumbs on all sides, then put them in the hot fat and fry until golden, turning so all sides are crisp and brown, approximately 3 minutes on each side. Serve hot.

FIG-ETABOUT IT CHICKEN

1 CUP RED BELL PEPPER STRIPS
1/2 CUP WHITE MUSHROOMS, QUARTERED
4 CHICKEN BREASTS SKINLESS AND BONELESS
2 TBS. OLIVE OIL
1/4 TSP BLACK PEPPER
DASH OF NUTMEG
1/2 TBS. KOSHER SALT
8-10 OZ UNSULFURED YELLOW FIGS DICED
1 TBS. FRESH CILANTRO
1/2 TABLESPOON CIDER VINEGAR
1/2 CUP APPLE JUICE
2 TABLESPOONS HONEY

CLEAN AND SLICE VEGETABLES. CUT CHICKEN INTO STRIPS 2" X 1/4". STIR-FRY CHICKEN STRIPS IN OLIVE OIL IN HEAVY SAUCEPAN OVER MEDIUM HEAT FOR 3 MINUTES. ADD ALL VEGETABLES AND SEASONINGS, EXCEPT FIGS, PARSLEY, AND BASIL. CONTINUE TO COOK FOR 15 MINUTES. ADD FIGS, PARSLEY, AND BASIL AND MIX WELL. ADD COVER AND COOK FOR ANOTHER 5 MIN. THEN…IF I HAVE TO TELL YOU, FIGATABOUT IT.

DECAYING DUCK

1 LARGE WHOLE DUCK (CLEAN IT)
1/4 CUP SALTED BUTTER
2 CUPS FRESH MUSHROOMS SLICED
2 CUPS SODA WATER (MINERAL WATER)
1 BAY LEAF
2 TBS. FLOUR
1/2 TSP POWDERED THYME
1/4 TEASPOON POWDERED CLOVE
4 CUPS OF YELLOW RUSSET POTATOES(DICED)
1/4 CUP OF UNSULFURED RAISINS

MELT THE BUTTER AND POUR OVER THE DUCK WITH SPICES. COVER AND COOK 1 HOUR AT 275F. THEN ADD MUSHROOMS, RAISINS AND POTATOES.
COOK FOR AN ADDITIONAL HOUR BEFORE SERVING.

Luciferian Lobster

Some say vampires are servants of Lucifer. Some say that vampires are the offspring of demons and humans. I really don't care, everybody likes lobster.

Get a big big lobster pot

Get 6 lobsters
Get a 6 pack of the cheapest beer you can stand
Get 6 big hot chili peppers
1 stick of butter
Dash of black pepper

And a dash of clove. Add water to the pot let it simmer then add the hot peppers, beer and a dash of cloves. Bring the water to a thundering hellish boil. Add the lobsters quickly cover the pot cook until lobsters are done (if you listen carefully you can hear them scream). Then melt the butter add the black pepper for dipping.
Serve it serve it serve it serve it enough already serve it! Delicious!!

Crabs from hell

Same as recipe above just substitute lobsters with crabs.
What'cha think…having crabs is special?

Rockin' Ruby Red Chicken

2 sprigs of fresh thyme
2 sprigs of cilantro
2 tbs. olive oil
1/4 cup Cranberry Juice
1 Tablespoon cider vinegar
2 teaspoons Kosher salt
1 cup diced red russet potatoes
1/2 cup diced fresh sweet red peppers
1/2 cup diced fresh sweet peppers
1/2 cup unsweetened hibiscus tea
3 lb. chicken thigh
3 Tablespoons Paprika

Combine cilantro, thyme, cider vinegar oil, wine and salt. Pour over chicken in shallow baking pan. Marinate overnight turning frequently.

Heat oven to 375 degrees. Color lavishly the chicken with paprika. Bake 1 hour then add potatoes and sweet red peppers.
Serves 4 or 2 very greedy people

Tastes Like Human Meatloaf

1/2 pound ground lamb
1 pound ground beef
1/2 pound ground ham or 1/2 pound ground dark turkey meat
1/2 cup finely crushed crackers
1 egg yolk
Pinch of cinnamon
Dash of ground clove
1/2 Tablespoon kosher salt

To make taste like human meatballs just mix the above ingredients, then mold into meatballs with a soup spoon. Place them on a cookie sheet. Bake in a preheated oven at 350 for 15-20 min. or until done.
Do not invite forensic investigators to dinner
Serves 4.

Black Death Eggs

4 cups of water
1 tablespoon Kosher salt
1/2 Tablespoons chopped licorice
8 large uncooked eggs
6 tbs. black caviar
1 tablespoons black seaweed salad finely chopped (you can find it in Korean or Japanese markets)
1 tbs. mayonnaise
1 tsp freshly ground white pepper

Add chopped licorice, salt and water add eggs still in the shell. Boil for 10 min. Then lightly crack the shell with the back of a spoon. **WITHOUT PEELING THEM** ... Place them back in the water and cook for another 5-7 min. Remove eggs from pot and let cool. Then shell the eggs, cut them in halves, and remove the yolks. Mash these well and combine with the remaining ingredients. Fill the yolks with the admixture chill till ready to serve.
Serves 8 people or 4 really greedy ghouls.

DRINKS AND SPIRITS

Changeling Chai

Will this make you a changeling or will it enable you to spot these creatures walking amongst you? It's for you to find out, I am sworn to not divulge anything more.

3 cups spring water
5 whole cloves
4 whole black peppers
2 sticks cinnamon
1 dash nutmeg

Bring these to a boil; let stand as long as possible. Then add:

1/4 cup loose black tea (or 4 tea bags)
Let steep. Then add:
2 cups milk

to the tea-spice mixture and heat but do not boil. When hot, strain and add:
1/4 cup of honey

What you need more instructions? Place chai into nice pretty cups ones with pretty leaves on them. Drink this mixture while sailing backwards on the Arctic seas, avoiding mermaids and sea wolves.

Goth Girl Mellow Tea

After a night of bloodlust and letting this will soothe your soul.

6 Cups water
1/2 Tablespoon Lavender
4 Whole cloves
1 vanilla bean

Bring these to a boil let steep for 10 min.
Strain and drink with honey; add cream if you wish.

Can also be served as an ice tea.

Do not operate heavy machinery or sign any legal documents after drinking this tea.

Do not think yourself wise and capable of turning into mist or a bat. The lavender impedes such abilities as it can be a tad bit of a relaxant.

Hibiscus Tea

For each portion of tea desired:

4 Tablespoons dried hibiscus flowers
6 cups boiling water
Honey (optional but strongly desired)

In a clay or porcelain teapot (a nonmetal pot), combine hibiscus flowers and boiling water.
Let stand for 10 minutes. Strain.
Serves 4-6.

Rotten Graveyard Coffee

Some types of vampires are known to haunt the graveyards. What does this have to do with coffee? Absolutely nothing, but the turmeric yields
an interesting pechunte flavor for the coffee.
When you add cream and sugar it looks like the color of decaying flesh. But don't take my word for it make a cup today!

1/3 cup Ground coffee
1/4 teaspoons Freshly ground nutmeg
1/2 Tablespoons turmeric
6 cups cold water

Place coffee in filter in the brew basket of the coffee maker. Add water where the water belongs in the coffee maker. Make sure the coffee maker is plugged in. Umm brew the stuff. Makes one serving.

This is good rotten coffee. If you do not believe me then I cannot help you.

Black Death Coffee

This coffee has a sedative effect while keeping you nice and awake.
This coffee has a stimulating effect while keeping you nice and sedated.

4 Tbs.. Ground Coffee, any variety
1/2 Tablespoon espresso
1/4 teaspoon powdered cloves
Dash black pepper
1/4 teaspoon Valerian
4-1/2 cups cold spring water (makes the coffee taste better)
cream and sugar to taste

Place coffee in filter in the brew basket of the coffee maker add valerian and black pepper.
Prepare coffee with cold spring water.

Do not operate heavy machinery while drinking the coffee or after.
You have been warned

Incubus Ice Tea

Seduction with a sweet flair.

6 regular-size tea bags
2 cups boiling water
8 cups cold spring
Granulated sugar or other sweetener to taste (optional)
1 12 oz can concentrated Frozen grape juice
1 cup pomegranate Juice
Pinch baking soda
3 x 3 Edible Gold Leaves

In a glass measuring cup or ceramic teapot large enough to accommodate the boiling water, place the tea bags and baking soda. Pour the boiling water over the tea bags. Cover and let steep for 15 minutes. Remove the tea bags and add grape juice. Pour the concentrate into a two-quart pitcher and add the cold water and edible gold.

Chill and serve over ice.

Apricot Cider

4 12 oz cans Apricot nectar
4 cups apple cider
1/4 cup dried unsulfured apricots
1 slice of ginger size of your thumb
1 cinnamon stick
1/4 teaspoon ground nutmeg
dash black pepper

Combine the ingredients in a slow cooker. Simmer on low until heated. Stir and serve.
Why not apple cider? Everyone knows how to prepare that and Apricot cider is tasty and nutritious, good for putting hair on elbows.

Yes!

DESSERTS AND OTHER DARK TREATS

Ice Cream & Sorbet

For these recipes you will need an ice cream maker. There is no getting around, it use an ice cream maker.

Lavender Ice cream

Lavender was a popular herb in the courts of King Solomon this ice cream is a delicious way to satisfy and calm most immortals.

6 1/2 cup heavy cream
2 teaspoons Dried Lavender flowers
2 Tablespoons HOT water
1/2 Cup shredded white chocolate
1/8 tsp. Salt
1/4 teaspoon vanilla extract
1 cup sugar

Crumble the lavender into a bowl, add water set aside for 10-15 minutes. Then combine heavy cream, Lavender, salt, sugar and. Freeze the ice cream in an ice cream maker according to the manufacturer's instructions and serve ..

Honey & Yogurt Ice Cream

Honey is the collective vomit of 1,000 of bees. Some vampires were known to vomit and consume blood. Doesn't this sound delicious?

4 cups unflavored yogurt
1 cup honey
dash white pepper

Put the yogurt and honey into the ice cream machine and freeze. Makes about 1 quart.

Moon Melon Sorbet

1 cup honey
1 cup water
1 1/2 cups pureed watermelon
1 1/2 cups pureed cantaloupe
1/2 cup Pomegranate Juice
pinch of allspice

Combine sugar, water and honey in a saucepan. Stir until it boils. Reduce heat and simmer for 5 minutes. Let cool. Refrigerate. Remove meat from the watermelon and discard seeds. Puree in a blender. Freeze the ice cream in an ice cream maker according to the manufacturer's instructions and serve.

Pomegranate Ice

4 1/2 cups Pomegranate Juice
1 1/4 c Sugar
1 teaspoon saffron

Combine water, sugar, juice and saffron in medium saucepan. Bring to a boil on medium heat, stirring constantly. Remove from heat and allow to cool. Pour mixture into canister of ice cream maker. Place in ice cream maker and follow the manufacturer's instructions. Makes 1 quart, approximately one serving.

Ginger Ice Cream

Ginger similar to Laudanum; it keeps the blood warm and adds a nice zing to any vein.
Unlike Laudanum it will not kill you or make you vomit your intestines out. Yummm...

1/3 cup water
1/4 cup finely pureed or grated fresh ginger, packed
5 large egg yolks
2/3 cup granulated sugar
1 cup whole milk
1 cup heavy cream
1/4 teaspoon salt

Combine the water and ginger in a small saucepan. Bring to a simmer over moderate heat, and simmer for 5 minutes. Remove pot from the heat and set aside. Beat the egg yolks with the sugar until thick and pale. It will start to swoon and cry out from the whisk. Set aside. In a saucepan combine milk, cream and ginger; bring to a simmer. Slowly add about 1/4 cup of hot milk mixture to the beaten eggs, whisking as you pour. Immediately add the tempered egg mixture into the hot milk mixture, whisking to combine.

Refrigerate stirring occasionally until cool, about 30-45 minutes. Freeze the ice cream in an ice cream maker according to the manufacturer's instructions and serve.

Real Ripe Red Raspberry Sorbet

Rrrrr ..

2 pints raspberries, washed and hulled
1 Cup Honey
1/4 cup Pomegranate Juice

Pour the raspberries in a food processor. You should have about 3 cups. Stir in 1 cup of the simple syrup . Taste and add remaining syrup if necessary. Place in ice cream maker and follow the manufacturer's instructions. Makes about 3 1/2 cups.

Dracula Sorbet

It is very ghood not blah blah bland

4 ounce unsweetened chocolate, broken into chunks
1 1/2 cups sugar
1 tablespoon chocolate syrup
1/2 cup diced maraschino cherries

Use a knife or a food processor to chop the chocolate into very small pieces. Heat the water and sugar together in a saucepan. Add the chocolate and simmer for 20 min. until the mixture is very smooth. Do not boil. Cool thoroughly add the cherries. Or if you do not want the cherries do not add them. Freeze the ice cream in an ice cream maker according to the manufacturer's instructions and serve. Freeze it next to the human heart you have in your freezer. Makes 1 quart.

Vetala Sorbet

Vampires, with their hands and feet turned backward, can reanimate the dead. It is unwise to run a race with them in this state, because their feet are backwards.

Vetalas are vampires. They like mangoes, honey and pomegranates amongst other things. I know because I asked one.

1 cup honey
1 cup water
pinch of saffron
4 ripe mangoes
1/4 cup pomegranate juice
teaspoon salt
teaspoon fresh ginger
dash of allspice
1 3x3 edible gold flakes

Peel and pit the mangoes. Pour in a food processor. You should have about 3 1/2 cups. Stir in the honey and water and pomegranate juice. Force the mixture through a fine sieve Pour the mixture into the bowl of the machine and freeze. Makes about 1 quart.

Count Von CocoSteinbabe Cake

If chocolate kisses could be like surfing on a pillar of bones and flesh.
If kisses could be like finding your neighbor hung in a cabinet for jerky.
If if if if if if if...
Alas, none of it can be.

This is a good cake.

1/4 cup olive oil (need I explain not to use Sunflower. I think not.)
1 tablespoons softened butter
4 squares unsweetened 100% GERMAN chocolate
3/4 cup water
1 cup sugar
1 egg, slightly beaten
1 1/4 cups all-purpose flour
1/4 cup powdered sifted unsweetened cocoa CO Cocoa. Damnit not instant hot chocolate...I know you...slacker.
1/2 teaspoon salt
1/2 teaspoon baking soda
1 teaspoon vanilla

Preheat oven to 350°. Heat oil and unsweetened chocolate in a pan on low temperature till chocolate is melted, about 3 to 4 minutes. Add water, sugar, egg, cocoa, flour, salt, baking soda, and vanilla. Using a fork, beat until smooth and creamy, or until you have finger cramps. Bake at 350° for 35 to 40 minutes, or until a wooden pick or butcher knife inserted in center comes out clean. Serve with severely whipped topping.

Pound of Flesh Cake

It is not true...
I did not do it, you can even ask the neighbor's cat; he will speak on my behalf.

2/3 cup butter
1 1/2 cups sugar
2 eggs
2 cups sifted flour
3/4 teaspoon baking powder
3/4 teaspoon salt
2/3 cups half and half
Pinch of clove
3 Pinches of French lavender ground finely

Cream butter and sugar until light and fluffy. Add eggs beating them like the wicked children they could've been had they made it past the ovum stage. Sift together the dry ingredients. YES THE DAMNED LAVENDER TOO!! Add sifted ingredients to creamed mixture, alternating with milk and vanilla. Pour batter into a greased and floured loaf pan. Bake at 325° for about 1 1/4 to 1 1/2 hours, or until butcher knife comes out clean.

GINGERBREAD HUMAN

CHEAPER THAN A VOODOO DOLL
AND NO PINS NEEDED...YUMMY

2 3/4 C. FLOUR
1/2 TSP. SODA
1 TSP. GINGER
1/2 TSP. SALT
1/2 C. SHORTENING
1/4 C. BROWN SUGAR
3/4 C. MOLASSES
1 BEATEN EGG
1 TSP. HOT WATER
1/2 T APRICOT JELLY
PINCH OF FINELY GROUND MYRRH.

MIX ALL INGREDIENTS. ROLL ONTO WELL-FLOURED SURFACE. HIT IT! HIT IT HARD WITH THE ROLLING PIN.... DAMN MONSTERS!!!

CUT INTO GINGERBREAD MEN. PLACE ON GREASED COOKIE SHEETS DUSTED WITH FLOUR.
BAKE AT 350 DEGREES UNTIL BROWN.

COAGULATED BLOOD

This recipe is good. Perfect for when you are tired of hunting an devouring your victim but need the same vibrational rate as blood.

Some of the alchemical and herbal elements of blood are contained within this delicious dessert: hibiscus which in some cultures is a symbol of blood and fertility, pomegranates which are symbols of immortality and honey. Finally, gold and silver traces of which are found in human blood.

All of these ingredients are sweetly suspended in a plasma like mixture called Agar-Agar, which is a form of seaweed. Some of the salts found in seaweed are similar to those in human blood.

This is good eating. This is almost as good as the real thing. Almost.

1/2 CUP COOL WATER
1 TABLESPOON AGAR FLAKES (1/2 TABLESPOONS IF IT IS AGAR POWDER)
1 CUP POMEGRANATE JUICE
1/2 CUPS HIBISCUS TEA
1/2 CUP HONEY
1 EDIBLE GOLD FLAKE 3x3
2 EDIBLE SILVER FLAKES 3x3
PINCH OF SEA SALT
PINCH OF MYRRH

PLACE ENTIRE MIXTURE IN A POT. LET SIT FOR 20 MINUTES. SLOWLY HEAT AND GRADUALLY INCREASE THE HEAT. STIR TO DISSOLVE STIRRING WELL AND CONTINUOUSLY UNTIL ALL THE FLAKES HAVE MELTED AND THE MIXTURE IS HOT AND THICK. REMOVE FROM HEAT WHEN THE MIXTURE IS VERY THICK AND ALMOST AT A BOIL.

Pour into 4 small cups. Place in refrigerator until solid. Any leftovers can be frozen for future use.

Some may enjoy this mixture before it has cooled into a solid. Letting it cool then freezing is better storage. It is up to you.

Enjoy.
This is the last recipe in this book. More cook books and guides **ARE FORTHCOMING...BUT ONLY FOR THE IMMORTAL**

INDEX

A
Appetizers 8

C
Cake
  Count Von CocoSteinbabe 50
  Gingerbread Human 52
  Pound of Flesh 51

D
Drinks 38
  Black Death Coffee 42
  Changeling Chai 39
  Goth Girl Mellow Tea 40
  Hibiscus Tea 40
  Incubus Ice Tea 43
  Rotten Graveyard Coffee 41

I
Ice Cream
  Ginger 47
  Honey & Yogurt 45
  Lavender 45

S
Sorbet
  Dracula 48
  Moon Melon 46
  Real Ripe Red Raspberry 48
  Vetala 49
Soups & Stews 15–26

T
Tartar
  Chicken 14
  Mermaid 12

SPECIAL THANKS

Robert Tynes
Alyn Cornell
Wheeler Clemmons
Chandra Batra
Victoria Ball
Heather Stockwell
Delinda Labeet
Peyton King
Richard Pareles
John Leonard

Changling Chai ~ Leah Barrows

Waiting for Starlight ~ Leah Barrows

ABOUT THE AUTHOR

Leah Lopes-Gonsalves Barrows is a mixed media artist, jewelry designer and lead singer of the gothic rock band Tung

(myspace.com/tung). The band Tung was listed as number 3 in WMFO FM's list of top ten bands in 2002. Leah has studied under former vogue photographer Robert Tynes and is now happily working in her private art studio. Leah can be reached at spiderscloset@yahoo.com. Her second book shall be coming out in October 2009.

Vampire with Urns ~ Leah Barrows

QUICK ORDER FORM

QUANTITY DISCOUNTS ARE AVAILABLE ON BULK PURCHASES OF THE VAMPYRE COOKBOOK FOR EDUCATIONAL PURPOSES, FUND RAISING OR GIFT GIVING. SPECIAL BOOKS, BOOKLETS OR BOOK EXCERPTS CAN ALSO BE CREATED TO FIT YOUR SPECIFIC NEEDS.

PLEASE CONTACT US FOR MORE INFORMATION

EMAIL ORDERS: VAMPYRE@PIRAASPUBLISHING.COM
FAX: (202) 832-0874
PHONE : (202) 506-3468
WEB PAGE:: HTTP://WWW.PIRAASPUBLISHING.COM

To order The Vampyre Cookbook, fill out the information below and mail it with your payment to:

PIRAAS PUBLISHING
PO BOX 29047
Washington, DC 20017

NAME: _____

ADDRESS: _____

CITY,STATE,ZIP: _____

COUNTRY: _____

Please send the following number of books:_____Qty
Price: $16.95

Shipping by Air:
US: $3.75 for the 1st book, $2.00 for each additional book.
Canada and Mexico: $5.00, Other countries $12.00

Credit Card Orders available through PayPal
paypal email: vampyre@piraaspublishing.com

www.ingramcontent.com/pod-product-compliance
Lightning Source LLC
Chambersburg PA
CBHW021026090426
42738CB00007B/924